RS

WITHDRAWN

Sestina for a Far-off Summer

Poems 1957–1962

– – – – –

–––––

SESTINA FOR A FAR-OFF SUMMER

POEMS 1957–1962

RICHMOND LATTIMORE

Ann Arbor • *The University of Michigan Press*

811
L356s

Copyright © by The University of Michigan 1962
All rights reserved
Library of Congress Catalog Card No. 62–13452
Published in the United States of America by
The University of Michigan Press and simultaneously
in Toronto, Canada, by Ambassador Books Limited
Manufactured in the United States of America

— — — — —

TO STEVEN AND ALEXANDER

138852

- - - - -

ALLEGHENY COLLEGE LIBRARY

Some of these poems have appeared, copyrighted, in various magazines, to all of whom I am indebted for permission to reprint, with occasional revisions. The poems in question have appeared as follows:

BRYN MAWR ALUMNAE MAGAZINE: The Watches

BRYN MAWR REVIEW: Well-head

GREENSLEEVES: Early Apples

THE GRIFFIN: Collages and Compositions

HARPER'S: The Academic Overture

THE HUDSON REVIEW: Goodbye Summer Goodbye Goodbye, Apologies to Creston, Remember Aphrodite, A Siding Near Chillicothe

THE KENYON REVIEW: Poussin's World, Andritsaina Revisited

THE NEW REPUBLIC: After Christmas, Arms and the Man, The Roman Soldier, North China and the Children, Details from the Nativity Scene, Problems of Disposal, A Lodging for the Night

THE NEW YORKER: The Krankenhaus of Leutkirch, copyright 1960 by The *New Yorker Magazine*

THE PENN QUARTERLY: The Crabs

POETRY (Chicago): Three Greek Virgins, The Pillow and the Book, Green and White, Mourning Doves, The Painter's Eye, Easter, Remorse, Failure, The First Seven Years

POETRY NORTHWEST: A Theme from Thomas Hobbes

THE TIMES LITERARY SUPPLEMENT (London): The Gulf Stream

Acknowledgement is also due to the following publications:

BEST ARTICLES AND STORIES: A Siding Near Chillicothe

NEW POEMS BY AMERICAN POETS, edited by Rolfe Humphries (New York: Ballantine Books, 1957): Max Schmitt in a Single Scull, The Father, Ship Bottom

— — — — —

Contents

— — — — —

— — — — —

I

- - - - -

Ship Bottom

How gay those bulks that tattered,
years gone, the lace of the blue giant. How gay,
in the Gulf Stream's film of pale calm, scattered
sea monsters at play
off the V of the prow's cool move. Now, shattered,

the giant's toys rot, sanded
and strewn. Oak ribs brown
in air, re-enact on dry water the landed
whale's grin and gasp, as if speared bulks drown
for sky in the lungs and die stranded.

Ship bones commemorate dead huge toys hurled
ashore by angry blue, time
sands their smash. Far out, still, leviathans, swirled
in the swim of transatlantic tides, climb
the arc of the world.

Black robes, hoods gold scarlet purple, bright heads
and old beards, the young pacers and the bumbling feet of age
unite now under ceremonial musics, or *gaudeamus.*

Let us rejoice then in our prime, while how well still
the gown molds the young wrestler's arms, how comely
blonde on black as youth models the robes of learning.

Somewhere about the middle of the procession
I thought, too, how our autumnal heraldries
glow upon the bulks and husks of the elders

to paint a rubric, red and black, on the folios
of forever; while all these stalks strengths flowers
shall be, in some sense, blown heads and florist's litter

swept into bins, and too soon. Or would it be rather
that the dignity, the enactment, the ceremony,
the time in June is eternity established? And through it

unchanged brush the light feet and young voices behind where
    ponderously
the brasses blare and basses deeply deliver the everlasting
gaudeamus igitur of the elder students.

How shall the river learn
its winter look, steel and brown, how shall we
upon our moving mirror here discern
the way light falls on bridge and bare tree
except as in the painting? Cold fires burn

autumn into winter. Here still
the pencilled sculls dip, precise arms beat
the water-circles of their progress. Skill
arrowheads elegance. City Line to 30th Street
is forever, Eakins, your Schuylkill

and ours. What you have done
made us see what we saw. Thus our eyes
after your image catch the steel and brown
of rowers on the water, improvise
by you our colors in the winter sun.

February Loves

St. Valentine is gone with his sweet arts
that practice on St. Valentine's day.
How green our winter thoughts incarnate here
in cardboard chocolate and scarlet hearts
where courteous lovers put their loves away
in attics for another year.

Gone, gone the smiles, the pink wings, gone for good
love's cherubs with their silly little
bows. But our season's iconography
displays, a symbol dreaming in our blood,
the virgin of the forest pinned by brittle
glass arrows on a winter tree.

The Father

They say the phoenix arrives at the time when his father dies.—Herodotus

Once a gay wit, subsequently a wretched instructor
with his lilacs and pigeons painted for the Malaga bourgeoisie;
even these painted no longer when the unbelievable son

was thirteen, and the brushes handed to him; the little teacher
relapsed to being Señor Ruiz, father to one who will not
perpetuate the name of Ruiz, but goes as Picasso

after the warm mother he liked. In the new universe
of meager blue harlequins, angled cubes becoming
musicians, bitterly sharpened bulls, and naked

desirable shapes of what age makes for consolation,
where will you find the pigeons or the lilacs, where handle
the brown feathers of such a bird as fathered this phoenix?

With full acknowledgement to Janet Flanner's "Profile,"
Part 1, *The New Yorker*, March 9, 1957.

— — — — —

To whatever here is done
so do
as if it had been one
by you.

Else leave it to die.
Never
brush a summary eye
over

word lines stuck
in form
round, deep in a book
and warm.

Do not by these know
about,
therefore, also,
no doubt.

Gristle and sinew,
green thews
grow grafted in you;
or lose

in washed lies
all force.
If so, better truly despise
this verse.

The Line

Friends I saw standing in that desolate line.
Final formation. But what used them so?
Outfalls, irregularity, design
or dearth was it that dried their strengths to shells,
or is this only time's iron grace who crowns
his queens and kings, then stacks them out to die?
People like us, and faces that we knew.
It was more than the clock. For I saw too
some green and golden heads among the grays,
and flowers infiltrate the arranged gravestones.
To Armageddon and the game of bones
are guided all formations of our days.

Where faceless prows are ranked upon the tide,
the larvae of the transatlantic fleet
stiffen on those gray waters where they dried:
rats in their brains, and padlocks on their feet.

Stand there, alone and strong,
in your green grove on the hill,
the timeless grass in the meadow.
Think of your sweet unseen
druidess in her green
leaves. Think how still
arm and stride are young.
Fifty feels twenty-eight
and sixty throws no shadow.
Still you have come too late.
The time of year is wrong.

The warm country is here
and we are here, but the time
of the mistaken season
has hung our loves to dry
on the wind, without how or why
or rhyme or reason.

The green barn on the high
line of the hill is only
a row of sticks on the sky
line, ugly and lonely.

Shall we no more to these
woods, no more, where worms
spin their nets in the trees?
Day is a dream of forms
here in whose summer shapes
August color escapes
the hold of eye and sense,
and only memory warms
the thin lines in the brain,

the row of sticks on the sky,
the loves forgotten again,
and who knows why?

Oh, end it, end it. The rhyme
is bad. There is no song
in the thin lines. The time
of the year is wrong.

Three Greek Virgins

1. *Seen on Penteli*

In the gray corner, under the line
of the fog, there was a cold
spring, curbed; one contorted pine;
a hut of stones; one old

man bent by the wooden trough;
an icon windowed on a stone post.
The holy angle hoarded its thin forms, enough
to make an emblem crossed

in its own version of what Mary can mean
on mountains, somberly combined above
stone plain and sea: a weather queen
in a cross of wind and one gray shape of love.

2. *Resident by Mistra*

Here on the black butt of the mountain they spattered an angle
of the Morea with their strongholds, so galvanized East to West
in feudalities of stone. How here to disentangle
Villehardouin from Paleologues? That hawk's nest

of a keep tumbled on the crest armored the Frank's baron,
while they below of the thunderous, the now crashed and sunken,
    lizard-written hall
fought him, sword to axe in the bloody defiles, pounded him from
    his warren.
Saints fade their eastern look on the murals now. South down the
    mountain wall

the Pantanassa crosses her convent in cypresses, serene
strokes on white plaster where nuns are alive next the welter
of wrecked chapels. Beyond, the staggering slopes lean
up into air angels live in, and by St. Barbara's shelter

peoples of the plain ascend in processionals red gold and white
to splash one dawn a year with singing in the cold growth of light.

3. *Dominant over Mykonos*

Lady of the open and the closed
waters: blessing from the points of your hills the little
    ships
leashed in the quiet of jetties; as, too, barques tossed
in the straits' fury, blown chips

miserable in storm: Mary of the Sea, who—with atten-
    dant Maries
and saints, Elmo and Elias, all who indwell
on the sloping wind those white-candy sanctuaries—
hold as yours this island, breakwater, beacon, harbor bell

and buoy: abstraction of sweet weather: for boats that ride
gray storm as green calm, possessively
throned on cliffs, whose sainted heroes burn at your side:
anassa: despotess of islands: queen of the sea.

— — — — —

That day she moved with her smoke, for what wind blew
dallied astern, ripples glassed, stayed with her, and seemed
to mold a sleeping ark, and brown weeds grew
and waved softly in the water; turtles dreamed

supine as scarabs liquidly engemmed
in blue motion, but slow, but slow; the whales
were black gestures miles off, and sharks gravely stemmed
their turns as long green sheaths with arcs of tails.

Fish were not real. Daydream, they seemed to say,
daydream, and gulls were thoughts, and what wings flew
those airs were loves seen lightly, when that day
stopped world and water in one spell of blue.

ALLEGHENY COLLEGE LIBRARY

Now, as the stripped tree lying in the corner, the tinsel
globes and stars packed in the box, and the pretty paper
piled at the top of the cellar steps remind us

that the child and shepherds are put to work and the
   philosophers gone back
where they came from, now, morose, too late as usual, let us
reconsider what growths may be coming to bud behind those
   winter

roses and steels, those cold gray masses that huddle our sunsets.
Yeats and Auden, sages among us, restive and sensitive, flared
their nostrils to some taint of death in the wind blowing

over Bethlehem, and the skies set for our re-enactment
glowed with such a wrong star as to confuse warm disavowal
that the beauty born under the year's heart might be somewhat
   monstrous.

Can worse than iron be muttering at the thunder-colored
edges of east? Have the peculiar priests, the scholarly murderers
dreamed up some new swallow-all and lemming-drive of
   destruction?

Let the language of poetry for once square off, try to
face the pragmatical, preposterous pig which Berkeley's
shining tissue of intellect could no more make disappear

than wishing will build us walls for our children. Still, what
   the world needs
most is philosophy, ever since the mythical magi
saddled from the manger and rode back into the cold desert.

— — — — —

A Theme from Thomas Hobbes

Theme and Garden

If memory is decayed sense, and imagination
is decayed memory, what do you make of you
or what do I make me, seeing I am
what I have seen, mostly?

                                    And now decayed.

As, item, in the muddy garden kneels
a woman, nineteenth-century Greek, half draped,
marble, I suppose, and the head knocked off.

                                    Or, item,

the house, eyes (once the windows of sense)
fallen in, the paint on the veranda floor
chipped, and the boards sagging.

                        Item, too, the sofa
in front of the shed faces the street, is horsehair;
double Cupid's bows of hardwood frame the back,
and nobody would sit there in the rain
except with an umbrella or a straw
hat, or as he might pose, with one hand on
his hip, and the other on the broken neck
of the kneeling woman.

                        And the sense decayed
and that was memory, and what was left
    when memory
decayed too was imagination, and the musty smell
of the garden, which remember is you and I,
is faded sense.

Seal Harbor and Marcy

But how we woke those mornings in the sun
from tumbled sleep and careless strength.

        How feet
were fury on the sand and ran the surf,
or found our water, numb blue where it hit
the eyes, but green upon the understones
and scuttling hermit shells, too cruelly cold
to swim, but how we stunned that azure sleep
of rage and icy water
to gasp and wallow on Atlantic stones
so cold and clean.

    And how the green wood then
was wild with misdemeanors, every bush
screened some pursuit, and every forest pool
had country ritual, every crash in the trees
a panic of birds, or angels of the sense
embraced in air.

 How force went spendthrift then
and all our flowers were all for sale
for nothing all those days.

      And now the year
as angry wood fights upward and explodes
from some old sense that festered in the ground.

– – – – –

The Korean Mound at Peitaiho

On my North China Coast there grew a mound,
simply green ground
in a shape. When I was five years old
somebody told
me it held Korean ears. I forget all
the story, but some legendary Chinese general
so stored the trophies of his victory
deep in one bloody mound beside the sea;
and I could climb, sit, slide
all over this green disease
but knew what lay inside.
Now, buried under tons of years,
my eye of sense still sees
that mound coiled full of bright new shining ears.

Spring, never half so sweet as now nor ever half so sweet
again, now if never after, come spring come

with

tree trunks in pools of water, green rain and yellow willows,
daisy wheels and buttercups, meadowlarks and song-sparrows
come spring come

with

milkmaids and shepherdesses, colin clouts and morris dances,
may rings and tennis balls, white shirts and boys running
come spring come

with

broken hearts mended, wars hates and cares and fears forgotten,
green strength and careless love, lazy wits and shallow fancies,
spring, never half so sweet as now nor ever half so sweet
again, now if never after, come spring come.

Like dolls on their little mile
of sand they walked, hand
closed on a finger of hand,
in a silent struggle of doubt
of the facts of love. And they did,
and they thought. And it all went out.
A tick of a watch, and it slid
and was gone for good and all,
though glance cut through glance and smile
and gray gaze to incise
love's effigy in the air
of the mind, fix there
forever the facts of eyes,
the skinfeel, the circumstance
of marriage, the stuff
of the act that slips away.
To remember will be enough
if they can remember today.

But it's gone, it won't stay.

The composition was hard:
the lighthouse, strict as a fact
on the dwindling spit, and the round
rock in the silver slip, and the packed
sand gritting the heel
of the hand, and the still pines
stuck in the rocks, and the sound
of the harbor buoy beating over
water, and gulls in the air
gray circles, and lover and lover
walking like dolls on their lines.

– – – – –

O pin, nail, fasten the picture hung in the gray of the mind,
if there's only a paper bag, a stick
of wood for tomorrow to find.

But it's all gone blind, gone blind.

No, out there, in a wheel
of gulls over the scum
on the gray water, it's real,
it's true, some-
thing tossing, a chip
in the tide, a splinter, a peel
of rind, or a sunk ship
floating a bone in the air.
It was real, it was true somehow,
it was there, it was there.
Gone in the gray now.

It's over, you can go now.

Apologies to Creston

As I remember there were other travelers, too,
but no communication. At 2 P.M. and about 102°
there was a Burlington transcontinental in the station,

stainless steel, gleaming under noon gold. We, there alighting
from our tired Chevrolet, as at the wellside in the antique desert,
sought the oasis shade and the water; we, carrying

enough money to feed us and our car and get home
and no more; carrying the fragments of prairie travel, of last night
slept on the sidewalk in front of the church, next the weed patch,

somewhere nameless in Nebraska on US 6; now ventured
the little metropolis, and in the shining drugstore assimilated
glutinous malts and sundaes; and all about us the sweet-and-pretty

of a model town freshened, pressed starched and crisp, as for a wedding
or garden party; and we, shabby at the eyes from little sleep, not well
shaved, dry and hairy, foreign matter in their green lettuce.

How can we pick the towns and stops in the passage
of our life, stick each one like a bug on a pin, assemble
a string, and show them to our dinner guests? Yet of these stuffs are
    we made.

And even of ours, they; despite disapprovals; and if only
as something once under a fingernail, or combed out
of an eyebrow. No communication. But there we are.

— — — — —

Forward then toward evening, and the meal in the wayside weeds,
and the horse opera from the dashboard into late hours, which finally
tumbled us into the camp ground tented with boy scouts, somewhere
near Keokuk,

and another day gone, and in the middle of it the unshared oasis.
Now on the map, unequivocally between Red Oak
and Chariton, find the name: Creston, Iowa: and hope we have not
been rude.

Here a young woman with no clothes on, mild,
marmoreal, hairless, handsome, dignified,
decants into an equally undressed child
(too young to walk, yet soon to be pie-eyed)
splashed wine. Elsewhere, one naked nymph, astride
a satyr piggy-back, points a stately hand
out of the picture toward some rout implied.
Design, not myth, made it. So the brain-land
Arcadia dreamed in paint. Neither the rose
smelled nor the sweat of actions in this June
of life's sweet counterfeit which art bestows.
Goats, gods, girls, and babies, blissfully immune
to dirt, fatigue, and morals, still compose
their own debauched, cherubic afternoon.

Arms and the Man

Let us assemble the medieval man
at arms from the display in the show case:
here an armet, a sloped and snouted can
to help him keep his brains inside his face:
a lobster-plated gauntlet for the hand
which swung that ridged excruciating mace
cruelly couched on velvet. So, rise and stand,
bad baron in your steely carapace
invulnerable. But did no creepy grace
by breath of charm under green straw of hair
or white of the witch-eye leer upon your shield?
Could you stare down the gibber in a field
of germs, wash brains, or poison your own air?
Povera bestia. Just stand there and dangle your mace.

Wearing some kind of iron hat, armed to the teeth with
whatever weapons are latest, he has stood in some square from
occupied Troy to now: seen from outside, monolithic;

dreaming inside of Vermont, or the Abruzzi, or Yorkshire,
or his father's boats tied at the jetty, or his girl in the grass,
or he's some slab without dreams, how do we know? Still less does he

know whether he's an angel with a sword or a fiend with a fork.
Somebody stuck him where he is, mostly among enthusiasts
who would hang him by the heels and spit on his head if they could.

If you upend the poor doll, its eyes will roll.
                                                    Statuary
these figures are stationed across the colored countries and the years,
all much alike, but there has been no intercommunication.

— — — — —

Do you remember, Aphrodite, the sea
hours we had; sun gone green in water
lapping over knees; the stare of the offshore
boats at the beachward bodies bare
in the daystar beat and noon glare?
Do you remember arms hesitant, given,
squeezed in the sun; the long day divided between
us (o Aphrodite remember heaven);
hung between memory and fancy of future, in the still
air of our day owned in the sun and the sea?

Red froth, shameward parts of the body dismembered, blue
pain in the loins slapped out seaward, spittle
and waste in the slipwash grew
you at the fury of the heart enfoamed, chaste and bare,
o brittle divinity broken into beauty,
regathered there in the huge eyes, white stand,
dark-hair, rain-enwimpled grace
of girl imagined in brain eye and hand.

And oh, remember, Aphrodite, the shell
under your swimming feet, cool and all
alone on the long water. And lest our days
now in the gathering of gray, years drying on
us, gleam gone from the pools
and the light lost on the sea,
lest they inch us out and confuse, I hold the idol true
in the eye: so also you
deep in the hollow of your dream
Aphrodite remember me.

– – – – –

North China and the Children

Pond country, and when willows in their pools
dream and loom back the trail and tress above
that weep, or as lily-pads where frogs squat plump
and dense, or where ducks cruise and color slats
of water, and all still ponds in all still forms
bring back the pavilion on the lotus-pool
and the painted bridge, the river and its drops
slid down and pearled from the bent oar that rowed
my father's boat, when I was five years old,
there where the bastion of the city wall
broke like some antediluvian stony ship
at Pao-ting-fu above the water-flowers.

Not one North China brat lives with his now
self as his own twin, nor as such whose first
home was not a rented temple, who does not know
that graves are pointed mounds of earth, that bricks
are baked in country kilns where you can find
dead babies if you dare look, who has not ridden
donkeys with bells on strings around their necks.
How can they live like us, if they came alive
by vitreous plumbing and grew strong among
sanitary odors? That man never smelled
who has not smelled North China in her pride.

This is no matriculation to the rear.
All we once children find the willowy pool,
splash down, pull the surface back in over us,
and douse in that green jelly where we were born.
The stone arch painted his own dream and form
as glaucous oval where the boat slid through
and the child's hand trailed in wonder and water-lily
stems. But this is the nursery, and the bed-time

- - - - -

milk, and the never-time of the fairy book
greenly enciphered in the stone-grown heart,
and not the year's content, only what squeezes out
in drops shining, but part of a piece of now.
I mean not China, only me and us.

We, once the dowered barbarian in the land,
the Goth on the capitol, dream now sadly back
as heirs to a kingdom gone. At Pei-tai-ho
the mountains, the monastery cliff, and Buddha's
Tooth, and one inarticulate village lost
in a gulf of stone behind the Great Wall, portended
and met the sea, where Chinese fancy ended
in Lotus Hills and Tiger Rocks, against
the tea-and-cricket, the whiskey-soda names,
West End, East Cliff, Lighthouse Point, where
   the children
of missionaries and importers and the marines
dabbled their pale toes in the North China Sea.
How gone, how our feet stand now on no times.

Changelings with me remember what's no longer
ours, nor all enchantment. Once pneumonic plague
whitened the snowless freeze in the Gobi wind,
and dogs wrestled the top boards from their nails
on coffins for cold meat. The facts come home.
Not ours the beggar with no face, but think
how lady meant European, woman meant
Chinese, how we sat in rickshas and made
our runners race. They've pitched the Foreign Devils,
that's us, and fallen for new foreign devils,
worship the goblin Marx and the bannered face.
Little we deserved either, but let it be.

— — — —

Some of them loved us when we were little, and we
loved them again, and the love that floats from a gone
amah-and-coolie world could still be love
that burns in blue above the festered corpse.

Children we shall not go back where they hauled
the nets in surf, seined flopping silvers, where thick
black boats were beached and roped to skinny anchors
that smelled of dead crabs under which the child
dried in his bliss, or where the diver slid
past the medusa steering her cold blobs
as azure emblems of a sea now lost.
And still the lighthouse gazes from the cliff
toward Chin-wan-tao, but we shall not come again
nor to the stone arch nor the lotus pond,
no more. But Chinese bells are in our heads.

Pond country is in my mind, and now at New Hope
the willows on the towpath, and all still
waters mean return, and five years old; they mean
green swimmings of the children, whose now here
floats on a scum of nowhere, but is theirs.

– – – – –

2

- - - - -

— — — — —

Spider

Bright captures, wing-shimmers, facts
of heart, sense, and fancy, as material
dreamed deep in my organs, anticipate
futures formed and radiant, when all
experience dissolves, desperate.

I eat my memories. Stomach stuff
of life is caught, shaped, and spread,
and what it was in the air,
gone from the flesh of thread
as form stays there.

Pearls and strings, rainwash, once
silent furies, now cling
quiet on heart-shapen leaves.
Spider does not sing,
only sits, sees, eats, and weaves.

The Procession and the Box: A Tapestry for Valentine

Now rides in the sweet silly season, and a progress
of armed shapes assembles on the frozen moor
out the window, and the year comes again, heartless
in steel plate. Open the box and shut the door.

What we have is here: our sometimes and our whens:
our nevers: hope caught in a jar: the girl on
the shell on the sea and the butterfly in the lens:
ropes in the arms: the face against the moon.

And outdoors, the riders pace at their season in bright rains
down stiff brown grass across a melting field.
Do we know them: strength, grace, hope: and what remains?
Oh, what red hearts we wear behind the iron shield.

The bus driver from Megalopolis had washed
his arms in wine, Karytaina castle dropped from sight behind
his elbow, and we saw Arcadia, eager to set up as new

the picture village of the mind from my forty-mile-a-day young-manhood,
a place of arbors and window boxes. But between times, andartes
and Nazis had played their games with it. There's something

in a bony hill town sucking on the blood of its past
that holds the inwards of you like a cold hand. We then,
lords of our little dollars, dried in the mouth over the goat-chops,

best these people could skin off the stones of their slopes;
and the pretty inn was gone somewhere unmentionable. At what was left,
we slept, and grumbled. Next day was given to Apollo's

house on the Bassai of the gray hillside, since not one
tourist ever went to Andritsaina for Andritsaina. It's the antiques.
And George, the drunken guide with the flower over his ear,

told us returning how, where we walked, resisters had stood the prodotes
in a line and gunned them into open graves, with Christos Christopoulos
the lordly and gentle innkeeper of the days of my youth.

Nazis were bad: who else good, who bad, my God, who knows now?
There had been women singing once as with hammers they broke
stones, long ago, to make the new road. It is not yet finished.

And still the grace is there in street faces and the bones of the people.
Andritsaina offered a scrubby flower plucked from the hillsides
of the days of all our freshness before the world was made so evil.

- - - -

The Crabs

There was a bucket full of them. They spilled,
crawled, climbed, clawed: slowly tossed
and fell: precision made: cold iodine color of their own
world of sand and occasional brown weed, round stone
chilled clean in the chopping waters of their coast.
One fell out. The marine thing on the grass
tried to trundle off, barbarian and immaculate and to be killed
with his kin. We lit water: dumped the living mass
in: contemplated tomatoes and corn: and with the good cheer of
    civilized man,
cigarettes, that is, and cold beer, and chatter,
waited out and lived down the ten-foot-away clatter
of crabs as they died for us inside their boiling can.

Crèche star and lit tree,
bells in the snow
every year
model the nativity
and show the holy family
and all its angels near
before they go.

Begin with arrangement. Protagonists
who are, but did not act, serene in the center
stage, and either side half-choruses. To the left
the shepherd thralls, a congregation of gray lumps,
embarrassed in nailed boots and coarse hoods, shuffle
their feet, and worship dumbly. On the right, lordly
philosophers dedicate with grace their whatevers
of perfumery and jewels. The middle triad is man
mother baby: representing the virtues, as honesty
devotion, and yet again some humanity still not fixed
in the stream of perception: a future: an icy bud
sealing beyond the world's imagination the tangible
dream to come. Behind, hardly seen, tame animals
breathe and gaze.
              Outside in the street, snow falling.
A few loungers. Also, significant of the world of power:
which holds, but is excluded from a history
it knows is happening: the mercenaries loiter
on their spears: hostile.

Why was it first shepherds? They, on the stony
slope at night: lonely but grouped: not owning
in full the animals they watched: not cunning
beyond the strategy of the wolf and the sheepstealer:
bored and tired: who possessed never any youth

– – – – –

you could call youth. See, this is what the choruses of satyrs
attendant on the year-spirit's birth are become
in our time. With imagination but without words,
how could they see deliverance from the wind
and the watching, the ephemeral coziness
of the leather bottle, except as they did see it?
Fireworks, that is, and gaudy gentlemen
in wings and wheels of light and glares of clothing
who blew trumpets at them, and spoke, loud but kind,
and invited them in to the circle of the privileged.

And on the day when these shall slip their essence
of sturdy gray for sheer weft and fluid
shall it be into what they imagined as lords of the world?
To this there is not yet any answer we know.
Only, that there was never again so bleak
an air on the stony slope, after such apparitions.

Next had come the wise Kings: young men, strong
and thoughtful: possessors already: and the imagination
of their dreams were simple figures of holding. Therefore
they gave, so that the gleam in the gift might be given
them to keep: in giving, asking then. One said:
I know that every sack has a small hole.
Where I climb no goat can go, where I swim no fish
follow; what squeezes on the heel of the hand
is sweet for resistance to the shoulder behind,
and the force blown headlong into exhaustion is a glory.
I am so strong and wonderful, but I can count,
and when I have to begin to be careful, what shall I do
then?
         The next said: The world is a magnificence in my eye.
But what shall I do, Lord, to store my possessions?

How can I keep the fern under the pine, and the gulls'
wings silvering flight on blue water, how seize
and hold the long green hills? My eye would devour them
and grasping, worship, for what is religion, but every
man trying to fasten the fluid of his lovely youth that escapes
and paint his glory forever on one sweet day?
Death I hate, not so much bones in coffin as when
the wave shall break or the leaf spin down
red, and I am there, and do not notice.
Captures escaping wash always the young sense fresher
but when the dear wish to capture is gone, then
Lord, what shall I do?

                    The third said: He has become
I, for in the spoiling of muscle and sense-shock
the mind is left, and plump or husked, here the abstract
tissue of inward is more beautiful than body
or bone even: the structure of God in the proposition.
Materials are necessary, organs and coil of bowels,
soapy brain or blood's broth. Some odd slimes
make these flowers of thought. If they dry,
petals crumble. Yet, death I fear not. It can be reasoned.
What do I need with teeth, hands, or parts, or courage?
But, Lord, when the visible cord of connection
slips in the vise, will not hold, I tell you, when I
can no longer follow proof to proof,
then, Lord, oh Lord, what shall become of me?

I do not think any answer was given at the time.
It was more likely in some off hour of the next
night: jogging the way home:
tired, in ordinary weather, a dry star or two
up there, but no more rockets or glory: camels
grunting and clanking: conversation at a fag end,

– – – – –

and gone, each man alone. One saw
the sinew on the rack, the wonderful force,
dying on the tree speared helpless petering out
in the icon of the imagination behind his eye.
He remembered how certain barbarous people would not
let a pubic boy be one of the men until
he had killed a bear. The village caught a cub and fed it
huge: chained him: the growing boys one after one
blooded their spears: they cut off his head and nailed it
over the village hall and prayed to it: Great bear
give us your hairy strength, o bear, let us be warriors.
But what if the bear's head answered: You have used me.
Your innocence is gone, you have not cared
for what it is to be a bear. What is strength?
I am a dry head, you are sick.

                                                                One saw
a man holding an open sack and the dollars dropped in
and jangled: the blessing and the beauty
of the company of love sold and paid for.
He dreamed of signing a check for the winsome
collocation of properties of the world
he had made his in a garden for his own bride.
He saw caterpillars eating leaves of his tree,
flies dying on his pond, and clotted the shining, and the girl
mumbled between decayed teeth stories of outright
possession and whoredom, and he stood in the shoddy ferns
holding his money.
                               One heard, in another garden,
the cry of the mind's pain, doubt of faith, crippled
understanding, the awful *why?* And he saw a blackboard
   written over
with judgments, and the only one that made any sense
said $a = a$.

After such dreaming they spoke
together, saying: Surely, we are nowhere near our answers
but it is plain we shall not reach them single
nor by the three of us only. Saying also:
What stuffs we gave were too much less than our askings,
and: Our strong acts fail until we forget the actor.
We are broken coins of each other, whose ragged edges
without our match simply eat air. Do you
remember, the other side of those three, some stuffing
of lumpish shapes? Is there some glimpse there
of God we have not seen? But what were those three
we were called, star-steered, magnetized
to their worship? Was it a real baby? We
have been told of the year-spirit, the child
of the breath of thunder in the body of the girl
who is a blossom split from the dreaming clod.
Yet we hope these are not gods. Of gods, we have heard:
wise and strong, but being perfect they must overpower
us, or we defy them. Surely it begins
not with God, that is too far beyond us,
but in our fathers or our children, in our people
to whom we belong and of whom we are a part
as they of us and belong. There it may come.
So, riding in the ruins of their pride,
puzzled and hope-starred still the shining kings
have left the stage.

Both choruses have gone.
Now the protagonists rose and left their places
in flight before the final element
of this morality: the titans or the satyrs,
the supernumeraries of the world of power
facing loss. They came in pikes and jacks.

— — — — —

43

They had the village hooped. Streets crossed and fouled
on armors and despair, and swords were out
and poking. There were screams. Aloof, secure
the woman in her blue hood rode her beast
and held the sleeping baby whose calm weight
dreamed on the saddle as the bearded man
plodded beside. Back in the snow, steel reeked.
The foundering henchmen gibbered on their loss.
Where is the king? Where is the tyrant child?
Where is the bud from thunder and the nymph
born with his crown askew in the green vines?
Oh, where are our lost afternoons displayed
in careless love, our elderly pursuits
in the hot grass? Where is the infant king?
Their fury strangled in the bloody dark.
The sound died, and the echoes were lost in the snow.

So all are gone. But every year
the child comes. The simple see
the lit tree
the angels and the gifts and glory.
Every year
the winter story
plays. The spirit hovers near
in wise brains that know
their own unwisdom, how gifts change and go.
But every year
the child is here
in the ceremonial tree
bells in the snow
until the day even we
in the night shall know
and see
who we are and where we go.

— — — —

Sweet fiction, flown now as material
in motion, now a shape made out of airs
and graces, you are heard along the hall
in songs, as footsteps up and down the stairs,
or, child, you are composed where arm and hand
lie in the vine's spilled shade along the floor,
or form from gloom of window panes to stand
and question shadows in the corridor.
Fragrance where flowers were none, echoes from where
no music made, o child, you lived from sight
as one small grace imagined on the air
who shrank to hide from the invading light,
but when the switch is turned you still are there
sucking your finger at my door all night.

— — — — —

Bed time as rain time drenched the homeward cars
who wiped and shifted at the corners, black
swam gold by haloed trees, wet lamps, flooded
shutters in glories, till they ebbed and drained
in rained-out hush, and the flat face of the land
turned toward an air now drying, in whose hole
of sucked-in silence at the mile-off yards
came locomotive time, and monsters barreled
in black walked out their furies, threw fits
of noise in pistons and reversed and stamped
their herds to silence; hooting, one long freight
puffed out into the prairie; on the void
came time of tick and tock and the loud clock
spoke through it and told how the unslept eyes
are cubicles for shabby transients, how
the brain ticks out nocturnal silence; now
gray seas softly stormed window panes, and there,
streets off, the milk-horse clopped his chips of noise
where hopped the morning rabbit on that grass
which makes the dewy time of oystershell
and hush filled with the rabbit and the horse
before tired sheets were thrown, and the night blind
came up to show, by grass and picket fence,
the world of the green walls, the backyard leaves
rainstrung and sweet from night and sung with birds
and dried in gold as the hot day came in.

She loves me she loves me
not in the white wheel and
fall, in the picked held and the
dropped petals; in watery
wind and blown weather she
loves me, and dry seasons
dry and she loves me
not in the stiffening
stalk time; on brown afternoons, think of long green
hours, through the cream-
y stripping of daisies she
loves me she loves me
not in the think times of
time, but in day time.

Use force and chisel, be lapidary, not
any cut-

stone-arranger. Fear finished counters. Take
splinters, make

grammar out of nails, paper, rubber bands
placed by hands

bemused, rags, pins, a piece of string,
anything

but ready-made lovely matters: Flowers,
whose rapt hours'

arranging builds on material
glory al-

ready shaped and sweet: pebbles: snow-
flakes are no

stuff. Not perfections. Only broken stones,
potsherds, bones,

scraps of felt pinched in a wire vise
can surprise;

or willful sense flash taken wrong:
half bird song

misremembered, shining phrase reworded
not recorded,

used, abused, retaken from the cannibal heart:
this is art.

– – – –

About a thousand years ago,
sick for lost love, sleepless alone I lay
from red dayfall through black to morning gray
trying to read *Ulysses* in a borrowed room
while yesterday's rejections played their act below
the ecstasies of Molly Bloom,

and the intolerable gray page
of print, in timeless nonsense, beat my eyes to mock
a lonely universe of sheets and clock
where I, king in an empty house and a night
cohabited by solitude and rage,
killed time into daylight,

and then got up, and left the place,
and never set eyes upon that furniture
again of white-night torment. O all poor
adolescents, what unsleeps you must endure, to span
with literature and life that deadly space
between the boy and man.

— — — — —

From the high deck of Santa Fe's El Capitan
cabs, sand-domes, stacks were seen above the box-car line:
old locomotives parked, antediluvian

in cruel progress, gone before us to that night
toward which we, sacks of memories, slide in blander airs,
and streamline our old eyes and thoughts from glass
     and flight.

Our ears, boys' ears, and eyes and hearts were haunted by
huge hoots of laughter down the dark: the glow: the steam
bulging in black and red up the spark-shot sky.

Now wheels, rails rust together, dews and sunshine eat
the iron grace: through silence their corrosion ticks
and drops in red dust, junk of grandeurs obsolete.

So, like old elephants who stumbled off to die
in their known place and rot their bulks from ivory bones,
the locomotives stood against the prairie sky.

Green and White

From and to Horace

Who sipped your drinks and saw Soracte bald with snow,
knew love sweet still, but knew too well how love's delight
goes where good Valentino and sweet Marilyn go
out at the cluttered dusty other end of night . . .

In which same night, this side, Horatius, I can see
the moths of hands and face make moments in the dark;
have my sweets still, but head gains over heart in me:
an elder wed to his Susanna, senior clerk

on legs as green as heron's, but the molting owl
glares from under my hat. Cut me and I'll still bleed.
But that thick pulse is watering into wit and soul
and reminiscence. Mine own vapors. Take no heed,

you by the hedge, and you who softly stroll and sit
and giggle in the half dark. Seize perfections, know
how the green time is still your own. Make use of it.
We did. I never thought how you could move me so.

No seed grew in the ground that year.
   That year no blade was seen.
The water sank in the dusty ground
   and no green tree was green.

And with dry hearts and brains of salt
   we hated the world we saw,
and neighbor stole from his neighbor's hoard,
   and no man knew the law.

The stone was dry in the spirit grove.
   The high gods heard no prayer.
The doubtful sphinx coiled in our hills
   and sickened all our air.

Then the Old Man came from the mountain side,
   down from the fields of snow,
with his stick and his beard and his dirty coat
   and the wisdom of long ago.

He told what songs to sing at the ground,
   what ribbons to hang on the tree,
and the wines to make and the kegs to break,
   and the rituals to let be,

and how to break the doom of the world
   and crack the fate in the glass
by setting back wisdom a hundred years
   and nature to where it was.

He made us dream on the youth we lost
   and the young dreams lost before,
when the memory-tree is green in the mind
   with leaves that it never wore.

— — — — —

He bounced the dance on the country green,
    and aped the teacher and priest,
and kicked the sergeant, and mocked the mayor,
    and drove the cook from the feast,
and the young grew wise and the old grew young
    and the great was less than the least;

and the high gods reeled on their thrones of ice
    as the red wine ran like rain,
and the rags dropped free of the Old Man's skin
    and his sinews were young again,

and the blood pumped in the dry of the veins
    and arm and fist swelled strong
and bright for never and white for now
    and beautiful for not-long.

For the man or maid who goes to the stone
    goes garlanded and gay
like groom or bride in pomp and pride
    with flowers along the way,
and the white bull dies with gilded horns
    upon his wedding day.

He ogled the girls, and chose his bride,
    and kissed her there in the light,
and hooked her waist in his giant arm
    and swept her into the night.

Nobody knows what went on in the hay
    and what went on in the clover,
but we found him asleep at the break of day,
    and the day-king's day was over.

— — — — —

We took him away to the private glade
   and the spiritual stone,
and stood him up, and broke in his head,
   and lopped him bone from bone,

and carefully sowed the reeking bits
   in the fields for miles around,
and the spirit worked in the rotting blood,
   and the seed grew in the ground;

and the fields turned sweet with glory of grain,
   and the young folk walked between
singing softly in the new rain,
   and all the new year was green.

- - - - -

Alone with verse I   made once, I, father   and blood spring suffer
haunt-wings and tease and   flitter of spirits.   These I have made, these
dream in paper, they   are: what fingers and   bone, what brain, what fat
of the loin, what lust   of the eye made, these   make now (undersleep
moves still memory   of unseen): bug-wings   glimmer and flitter
as rhyme and word-host   calling me father.   Alone with what I
made and am making   I, the red pump, pump,   and as gnats' thin wings
whine, and hovercloud   haunts me, the paper   indestructible
universe, that is   I and my poems,   mimes out the no-world.
Over the wellhead   wings whir and glimmer.

Again and again up there the apothecaries combining
ingredients repeat their reciprocal series
of experiments: shaking loose on the dance floor, at the community

pool the combinations of futures: soft looks, the connubial
expression in the eyes: it means squeeze, germination, cramming
the lovely confusion till there's no room, no room. Presently

room's made in a hotter kind of chemistry: holocausts
happen in hate: messes occur: red collisions, whenas
it becomes compulsive to sponge and wipe up certain congestions

on the bleeding globe. So 1914 1939 19 when?
Captivate and create, undo, clean up, and begin it
again. But if upstairs the apothecaries, bugging

their abominable eyes over the crucible, become
aware that material has eaten its own tissue, no more
combinations will ensue? One only surmises that, learning

nothing, they will pick up the apparatus and try it all again,
    elsewhere.

- - - - -

Early Apples

All week they had fallen, while on stones and grassed
ground we knelt to the circle of the tree
to gather hard bright balls, and at the last
it was down to weak blobs, leaking filthily

colored juice like chewed tobacco. So I stand
under the tree and rage at time and God
palming the wet brown smell in my clean hand.
O future, future. High above, the proud

shape towers to green still sown with rounded gold,
like some lost sight of the Hesperides'
domain. The world was apple. Pale and cold
our ciders juiced in such tight balls as these

before their rot, and shapes of innocence
and fresh delight were apples that grew young.
Globes were the skins of all experience
firming the damp pith, yellow sap, and strong

brown-buttoned stem and core, to show and be
the story of love undone, foul death foreplanned
where Eve stood in her hair beneath the tree
and held the bitten apple in her hand.

— — — — —

The names of birds are near
heart's heritage in our lines of song and story.
They will not leave our minds. These names are here,
and on these pages painted in their glory
the book-writ birds appear.

Wryneck, by foredone
or lovesick maidens fastened on a wheel
and turned by night and hidden from the sun
by day, and sung by moonlight, thus to steal
back the beloved one:

jynx torquilla, brown, barred,
and with the woodpecker's long toes to use
for climbing. He's Ixion the ill-starred
who rides his jinx-wheel, by the hand of Zeus
for love flung far and hard.

Bustard, once annoyed
by Xenophon's men on the Euphrates plain,
who ran with feet uplifted and employed
his wings like sails, and was not seen again.
Alone upon the void

the black *Imperial*
Eagle uses one head, yet once he knew
prerogatives of the armorial,
and on a Habsburg blazon he wore two.
Grandeur for him was all.

Lapwing, that Benedick's
Beatrice ran like. *White Stork,* long of life
and leg, who nests among the chimney sticks

and stones, and flies the baby to the wife
in spite of all our tricks.

Skylark, whose simple song
stirred Shelley into several thousand words,
though Huxley's D. H. Lawrence thought it wrong
to switch him from the company of real birds
into the angelic throng

that poet was so prone
to find himself projected in. There are
a few who see in birds the overtone
of Unseen Presences moving from afar,
not just the bird alone;

for instance, Wordsworth, who
from birds in general saw intimations
of immortality for himself, and knew
only some transcendental implications
within the name *Cuckoo*.

Fieldfare, once greedily
dined on by Cleopatra (that's from Shaw).
Nightjar, beloved of John Galsworthy,
looking most like a drowsy pile of straw
or whippoorwill to me.

From Thracian fairy tale
King *Hoopoe*, helmet crested, striped of wing;
Swallow, not here of barns; with her, a pale
brown sister bird condemned to grieve and sing,
the fabulous *Nightingale*

— — — — —

from prehistoric haze
of myth who bubbles still her tale of wrong,
the bright and bloody thread caught in a maze
of moonlight woods and legendary song
to haunt us all our days.

Kingfisher, not as here
shock-headed, but streamlined from beak to wings
to bolt his blue dive down the atmosphere,
whose nesting stills the winter sea and brings
the halcyon time of year.

Names, names of birds. Always where
books will be read and stories still will be
remembered, in a not too festered air,
bright and so literate for all to see,
the birds will still be there.

*A Field Guide to the Birds of Britain and
Europe,* by Roger Tory Peterson, Guy Mountfort,
and P. A. D. Hollom (Houghton Mifflin). With
gratitude.

— — — —

3

- - - - -

1

This is a world of picket fences, knowing
the girls pass arm in arm from up the courthouse square
down to the soda parlor, hears them throwing
the fragments of their laughter down the dark
and summer-close and elm-grown small town air.
The bandstand in the middle of the park
watches lank adolescents swing their cars
with languid fingers into cruel curves,
reverse and start and wipe the night with stars,
and take the road, this ribbon world of nerves
driving forever driving in a dream
of black escape from automobile eyes.
On either hand the backyard landscapes stream
as flight in fluid haste, and memory-wise.

2

A fallen column overgrown with grass:
a U-shaped lyre bestrides it, and the bust
of a baroque musician in a wig
observes your steps upon this antique dust.
A broken angel with a dizzy smile
invites you in; and did you know how big
flowers in our heart the classic world, the style
of swans in lakes, tutu and entrechat
and figure manual by Petitpas?
The lonely cemetery of the heart
grows on its graves and in its cracks of stones
such blooms as break the granite shells apart
where reminiscent ballerinas start
out of the sweet arrangements of our bones.

3

Knee deep in froth of daisies and the night,
you found the house, haunted the window light
thinned by drawn shade, and wetly stood and spoke:
"Let me back in, since I lived here before."
Your black key sickened in the lock and broke.
You could not force the door.
Steps sounded in the house and went away.
The moon came out and bleached a broken gate
where too much grass had grown. All you could do
was wait, count your lost pulse, watch the moon climb,
and try the hopeless door again, and wait,
while this night scene of all you could not do
enciphers you into the rest of time.
The story is not finished. This is you.

4

Noon sharpened every outline that you saw,
the braided sinews on the drawbridge gates,
the prison guard, rapt in his tower of glass,
the tarns of ice engraved with sticks and skates,
crows in the frozen cocks of harvest straw,
the tanks of heaters, stacked and stripped of gas,
white smoke, stopped on the blue, as frozen fleece.
Riding the slipstream to the edge of sight
it does not flow but slides in all one piece
back from the tunnel where you clipped the light
in snapping shears of stone and lost your day.
But lost is won nor gone is gone away.
All aching splinters of this day remain
and reassemble in the pondering brain.

5

Now day's bright angers glitter in the skull.
The lightless outer air is squeezed away
and makes a coffin of our wheeling hull
for these two hours as, lit within, and thrown
in the wrong way
and inside out from headlong panes, the play
of shadows gives ourselves to us, and mocks
our ghosts in glass, the slogans in a line
of platitudes below the roof, and rocks
the idiotic sisters on their sign.
Here in our small sealed universe we breathe each
   other's air,
companionless companions of the train.
We are the uncommunicated thoughts who stare
and jostle, cooped inside one iron brain.

6

Cased in such brains, the swarming parts of me
turned and grew inward, monads of the mind,
and as they died, each in his private, blind,
unwindowed consciousness, mold and leaf rot
worked in the reminiscence of the sense
and germinated in the iron pot.
I grow in my own landscape like a tree.
The glory shapes inside the grass-grown fence.
I wear this rainbow wash of dreams that make
a false imperium of pride, rehearse
my splendors in a cruel travesty, and shake
the helpless sovereign in his universe.
That thing is I. But what I try to be
I am not. What I am, I can not see.

- - - - -

7

Here stands the town, our castles in its trees
by whose dark involutions lie embraced
our rights and tithes, our franks and baronies.
Its theme, our lives, escaped in wheels and haste:
its streets, our parish where dreams feed like sheep:
the 1860 general in the square:
the flat boat on the river mud asleep:
the depot stranded in its ties and steel:
the stations of our time in everywhere.
The midnight park where sweethearts clasp and kiss
in leafy corners makes the witness moon
accomplice to our metamorphosis.
Our own eyes light behind the window frames
as bulbs and shades, and shine as private flames.

8

A pole of spine, a hatch of sticks and strings,
a cage of nerves hook up, suspend, and shore
my treasury of vapors, winds, and heat.
Somewhere in this neat wilderness there sings
the miniature of an angelic mind.
Inside the wall a whole wonderful wide
creation in full sovereignty maintains
the soft interior of pulps and veins.
Illuminated memory inside
this rhetoric of flesh, this more than meat
of physiology, grows inward wings.
In me and nowhere else the world is grown.
By which dear mess of waters, salts, and fats
my germ walks singing through its frame of slats.

- - - - -

9

The gift of giving countermands the loss.
Me: you: the boundaries blend, our private nights
with all their starry populations cross.
I give you mine with all its rents and rights.
If on the backs of graves we kissed and held,
the flimsy specters dallied in their sheets.
The driven progress of our flight compelled
fond fresh conjunctions in our midnight streets.
Sometimes such lonely spheres, adrift and blind,
wearing their glories in a sconce of bone,
trespass on miracles and wake to find
through soft collisions that they are not alone.
Dear love, take in my vase of star-grown flowers.
The door is open and the house is ours.

Shrike

As executioner, he wears
a mask across his eyes, and tears
his prey with hooky beak, and cares

nothing for victims' pains or cries;
impales his meat before it dies
on barbs and thorns against the skies.

He stocks his larder thriftily,
carnivorous almost as we,
a careful baron in his tree,

the terror of each smaller thing
that flies and nests. And in the spring
he falls in love and tries to sing.

Unwelcome Thrift on Judgment Day

How, when all we who breathe are stopped and sown,
compost to feed the nerves of grass and grain,
shall all the thoughts that bulge against the bone,
the wishes from the cocoon of the brain
half-winged for bright escape, be gathered back
while angry angels bugle home the yield
of all the world's best time, and stoop to hack
our reputations from their reeking field?
Domed of our joints and blood, our books and lines
of grace in shapen stone, our works of art
and civic strength, the city of heaven shines:
manifest future. And this heretic heart
resents his imperfections all denied.
Green grew the buds damned when the old tree died.

Roses cloud my arms in green, stick
and hurt; red climbs from stalk and water, flying
suckers arch; shears lop vain heads, my hands
bag and stack the lost splendors. Roses
hurt, delight, make me think of dying.

Roses, too sudden, dramatize
my birth and bud, scarlet and astonishment, in
    steep array
among the greens, rains, thorns, my
pride, spiky postures of defense, farewell
favors, fading glory, sweet decay.

Where where in rose time find some way
to keep and fasten, hold forever in the hurt
heart this June pain and passion? See
from dead-colored wood green wood swells: for other
    Junes of roses
spermy future updriven from the deep dirt.

Mourning Doves

Soft and startled out of wind carven slopes, the prairie lights
run them up and out in wind and sun, paired flights
of doves, fluid on the dry, as flying tails, browns and whites,

Utah to Connecticut two by two identical,
paired in flight, or modelling high breasted sweet symmetrical
sentimental shapes along the wires or country fence rail.

Wild mourning doves are all alike. Urban rock pigeons breed
hybrid multicolored gang-grouped citizens, they wheel and feed
in squares and parks, man-wise, dainty, vain, full of greed,

and no two alike. Messy marriers. City pigeons coo
but garble calls with mongrel-sorted colors.
                                        Two by two
identical to shape and in their little whoop and hoo hoo hoo

wild mourning doves are constant lovers ever to themselves and
   to their nature true.

Flags hang on the wall
limp as winds fall.
Barons stand blank and tall.

Dragons sleep in a school
of coiled wings, and cool
their mail in the garden pool.

Sweethearts fly in the air.
Angels sit on the stair
and comb their bright hair.

Unicorns in full view
graze groves and fields through.
The trees are blue.

Hand heavy, eyes of lead,
the king sleeps on his bed.
Dreams fill the white head.

The snake tooth pinches his own mail:
the rabid dog fox bites his foot:
cancerous claw and scorpion tail
turn inward and self-rend. Brute

crab in the box eats the lung.
He tears the fact, unmakes the made.
The pelican, who feeds his young
on his own flesh by flesh betrayed,

reverses beak to split the wound,
bites on the sack and pulls it through,
throws heart and vitals on the ground
to prove that heart, at least, was true.

Easter

Our April is the lamb who died
to paint the year in tones of pride
blown where the lamb was crucified.

The lamb was slaughtered where he stood.
They nailed the lamb across the wood.
They carved the lamb and boiled his blood.

How shall we pack our sins of pride?
The ruffling soldiers lounged and eyed
the carcass of the lamb who died
and speared the water from his side.

The glory of the year has grown
from where they buried the unknown
lamb in a hole beneath the stone.

Lilies blown in soft airs repeat
the victim killed, the lamb to eat,
the heart and entrails dressed as meat.

How could the time transform him so?
How did the lamb make April grow?
The lily and the blood root know.
They drank his blood beneath the snow.

Failure

How did it come ungathered, all the sheaved throng
of graces and good-byes? Dandelion-blown in the strong
wind, time's spindrift-whirling pressures, our young

moment of together and yesterday flies
the storm. The date enacts and dies.
How can I hold the look in your eyes?

How pull and store thistledown out of the blast?
It slipped, air-caught, at the last.
Sweet wind, sweet wind, where have you blown our past?

That was a time of furniture and family
and books and gramophones and happiness
and afternoon and servants and late tea
and lamps, my mother in a trailing dress,
the vases on the mantel white and blue,
the cat asleep along the window sill.
Our Victor with the morning-glory horn
held Farrar and Caruso in its walnut case
and bugled Marguerites and Butterflies.
The rainbow fairy books by Andrew Lang
with Eisenkopf and princesses forlorn
displayed their simple magics to my face.
The antiques of the heart can spell me still.
That wood was haunted and the bluebird sang.

December Fragments

I thought of cards along the mantelpiece,
the fire of logs, the stockings on the wall,
the team of deer, the cotton beard, the sleigh,
the ox and donkey munching winter hay,
the sleeping doll beside the floodlit stall,
shepherds and lambs in imitation fleece,
the sentimental chimney and the chair,
tin horns on earth and fireworks in the air,
peace and good will. Dear trash, I loved you so.
I thought of stars and bulbs and tinsel strings,
angels in curling pins, with paper wings,
bells of spun glass, and drifts of mineral snow.

Twin iconographies. The two young horsemen rear
their mounts above two fallen dark antagonists.
Each has his victim stuck on a down-driven spear.
St. George has pinned a dragon form who flails and twists
in snakish sprawl. Demetrius in the other frame
kills an unhappy looking bearded warrior.
Rider spear prey: the composition is the same.
Our fiends their fallen, and our saintly calendar
their acts, their history our hope, and still they ride
against the reptile rancor and the armored force
of fury, martyr and knight-errant side by side.
Each spears his destined terror from a heaving horse.
Dimitri I. The outer Frank or Turk lies still.
The poisonous snake's inside, too hard for me to kill.

The forest nuns, who sheltered us and healed
with charms and science our unfinished frames,
spelled us with some effluvium of the sense
from their own childhoods' wonderment concealed
behind the robe, the veil, the snowy shield.
We knew no tongues; we only knew their names,
identities, and smiles, could not communicate.
Yet all is of a piece; some essence still comes through
from the house, the sisters, and, outside the gate,
the gloom, the wizard world of pines, the great,
the haunted and inhabited and enthralled
interminable Würtembergerwald,
and I remember what I never rightly knew,
as in a harbored memory, not quite mine,
that German mind whose gothic dreams divine
the Kobold of the stream, the burnished ritterling,
the sylvan witch who sings behind her door,
the chilly jungfrau of the sevenfold spring,
and psychic manikins who with folded wing
sit on the mushroom circles of the forest floor.

They waken the weed-grown drums from their sprawl of death,
    pile up
columns, rebuild the anatomy of parthenons, with white plaster
caulk the cracks, new marbles are boned into the holes in
    the temples.

Persephone, Kore, doll of death in the iris, pupilla
butterfly-winged as psyche floating in the dust of the subter-
ranean hive above the squirming ribbon of snake; arid

is your transit: peaches wrinkle, apples blear in the salt wind,
oases shrink upon their cities and springs run sand.
Arrogant your return from the putrid sleep in the boneyard.

And houses die before the bulldozer, crumbled and carted
off, men work in the slats of doors to nowhere, naked
pipes are nucleus to the new nightmare of concrete uprising.

Some poison pains the physics of the dust to reassemble
and lust to sprout and writhe, and the potash cities rankle
as weeds in the living desert. Your April, Persephone,

resurrects in your walking. In hair spun and piled like butter,
mouth pouting, eyes like eggs, juice in all the tubes and the bulges
tight, the proud doll trips on four-inch heels down the marble
    sidewalk.

The Macedonian Chamber Tomb

My idiot's glory. Privacy conceals
the solitude of his confines who feels
only his roof eggshelled above and cracked
for life to fester in, the germ of addled fact.
Build me a dome
and break it. Such is my eternal home.
And in this buried belfry who but the bat,
that filthy mouse with wings who acts the soul,
sleeps off his fidgets hanging by his heels?
It only needs a hole
in the head for life to mold and rot the brain.
Sun breaks now in the roof-hole. None so brave
as this imbrained stone-hatted world of mine
where the chambered girl dreams through her
   golden rain,
and Plato's solipsists all in a line
chained to their endless television pine
for sky, and pull the world inside their cave.

The Interval

The room half lived in, the two beds, and one
is empty, and our clock guarding the shelf
wakes only me. I hold this shell of time,
this bubble of being, and am half myself,
and feed on fragments, charm the hours with rhyme.
Room, my arterial castle, how undone
you are through loss in being only mine.
Memory sleeps in my arms and I wake up
to the white imagination in the sheets
and cold promise of past. The filtered blinds
of dawn, the roosters heard far off, the streets
breathing sweet recent rain bring back the cries
that woke our sleeps together, when the world
was in one piece, and I could see your eyes.

A Lodging for the Night

Verona was always arduous. The station is colossal
and next to nowhere. No room in any hotel, they told us.
We stood stupidly in the vast halls, and the train was gone

into midnight. A fat dubious man and a sober thin one
murmured, it's the opera season, but spoke of a lodging,
bellissima, altogether respectable. They teetered the suitcases

on the handlebars of a bicycle. Walking half in our sleep
we trailed them past silent crowds of men sitting asleep on
baggage, or brushing their teeth into the empty cabstand.

We dreamed along dead beat down the bright enormous
desolate street. From a café a woman in a Garbo raincoat
got up and followed us a few steps shaking her head. It all came

out of some modern Italian movie. We shambled under
a gate, across a court. There was a clean shabby hallway,
an old woman and a little girl. I have no idea where they

slept. Our chamber was huge, the bed eight feet
wide, and hard as we lay and watched where on the dresser
across the room, a doll, large as a child, staring with solemn

eyes, waved forever still in the air her waxen expensive fingers.

Memory of a Scholar

(W. A. O. 1880–1945)

I set this down. Magister, can it be?
How shall I shape the wind that once was you?
Fancies seduce the memories in me.
This must be true, though nothing else were true.
I dared not praise you when you were alive.
Not I. You would have blown me off my feet
with stormy courtesy, the roar of wit
hiding the old Greek dread of godlike praise
for living men. But how shall verse contrive
your presence? Wave, my wand. So I recall
a Wilamowitz seen as Buffalo Bill, ·
Boeckh on a bicycle, and with it all
a better bibliographer by far
than any of your German idols. Now I see
the calligraphic hand, the blacksmith's bust,
the Civil War commander's brusque imperial,
the cavalry moustache, the chin upthrust,
the big bold pipe, the bolder black cigar,
the paleographer's fastidious eye.
You, my professor, you before my face
unrolled the script of scholars, put in place
Traube and Vahlen, Leo, Reitzenstein,
and set the stars for all our lives to steer them by.
Your force was schooled to skills, the leonine
turned lapidary; syntax and the line
at fault and needing surgery brought to bear
the steely grammar shaped in pain and care.
You mounted on minutiae to aspire
with Plato up the staircase of ideas
and ranged, a ruler, all his cloudy sky,
and came back down to his deep cave with light and heat

- - - - -

in worlds where men see dust and you saw fire,
to blow your edicts from your chair at ease,
Jupiter of the seminar benign
with poets nuns and Baptists sitting at your feet.

It was the river. Far away and late
I heard the story of the overturned canoe,
your call, "go help the others," and the great heart stayed
in death. Think of that country that we knew
so well, land of black woods and trailing vines
and inland muddy streams that held your fate,
the Pollywogs, the flooded Danville mines,
Sangamon and Vermilion and Salt Fork,
our professorial playground. How we played
beside the crawfish-catfish-haunted Lethe stream
through overall-and-gallus groves of Academe.
Sulphured for chiggers, through the green opaque
fills of the scoops we swam, and dried in air,
played softball in cow-pastures, fried our steak,
stood by the fire and rocked the night with corny song
and shone the moon with outlaw rye and legal beer.
And now you are gone out of a world gone wrong.
Spirit is storm. You can not catch and keep it near.
Verse will not hold you fixed. The river took
you, and your spirit on the plains
will shout with the old laughter over all my pains
to put a man alive inside a book.
End from an epitaph you turned me to:
the tribute to a Roman Spanish charioteer:
Now pour the wine. Your friends and flowers are here.
Never forget. For there was none like you.

Dramatis Personae

Wardrobes of empty doublets stalk the stage.
My chorus gathers wool and mutters what
is more like me than sense. The sad kings rage
and die their destinies. How do I rig
my thoughts to yours? We sew them in a knot
of noise and hooks of lines. Before the cardboard scene
the patterns of convention, the coiffed queen,
forever one-eyed knave, and frosty king of hearts
act their foreseen and necessary parts
to beat your nerves and eyes with what has never been.
How was the lie so tragic and so big?
The princess grieved for love and shook her hair.
Nothing inside. She spoke of passion so.
That lovely head was spouting from wild air.

- - - - -

On Monte Cavo a bulb of defense has sprouted. It masters
the mirror of the forest girl, the kingly branch and the oak leaves,
the pope's castle that was a hood of blessing above the waters.

We mooned on up as when we were young, Frascati to Tusculum.
Boy scouts in paper shields and swords of wood were enacting
games of Roman against Latin, very seriously

squatting in the ditch of the Cyclopean, the prehistoric
road to ambuscade the enemy. It was a feast day.
The Lambretta lover and his pillion lass were there in the bushes.

We strolled and stopped in the sacred forest once of our courting
days. Issuing late Latin winter sun warmed the strings
of knees and articulated the precise progress of ankles.

We sat for too-new wine in a forest of vats hogsheads
and spigots, giggling at each other across the greenish
stuff in the tumblers, silly as a couple of adolescents.

Memory becalms us, it shines. But in the green of our ice
there is a fly stuck. We can't get at it to take it out.
Pretend it isn't there and continue in hours translucent.

We inhabit a world jammed with old hates, black wrongs. The
    frame twists.
Monkeys men and mice are getting thrown at the moon and the
    planets.
What end who knows. We go on with our mature occupations.

Some middle hours of this life are lazy and blond as honey.

- - - - -

The old bus rattled downhill and stopped at the jetty. We got out.
Piles floated beards of moss in thick water. Holes
showed in the landing boards. Always we were docile. We stood
    there

in line at a table where the old man was sitting.
A brass stud fastened the soiled shirt over his adam's apple
and the silver bristles on his neck. With the stub of a pencil

he wrote our tickets one by one, painfully inserting
two carbons for three sheets apiece. It took half an hour.
Our careful feet rocked the boat as we stepped down on thwarts.

And it was too full of course. The motor stalled three times going
over. We all stood and smoked. It was too dark to see much.
(They had told us the boat and water would be full of brides

and babies, young men lost in battle, the wreckage of youth
and dreams and tears, glories foregone, bright loves forgotten.)
A rat's head ran out a slim wake that pittered

and plinked on the stones. Gray grew in that light the lilies
beyond the margin. Then in black water arms, hips, elbows
stirred, fattened to white, turned over and sank, as the keel slid

soft over flesh. Some hair, I think, streamed on that surface.
At the far side a few piles and planks were sketched. Here
as we lurched ashore one by one the grubby old hand

accepted, once now and forever, the shabby stubs of our tickets.

Sestina for a Far-off Summer

We cradled the heavy green canoe in our arms
and walked it down the steep path to the river.
To launch and land the weight was all our problem.
We stormed the current (how the arms of youth
are strong) and found our beach below the forest
golden in early afternoon of summer.

That was the careless story of all our summer.
Sun was warm gold and water sweet on arms.
We changed and dried behind the ferns in the forest.
Our private sandy beach far up the river
was bright with laughter, blond-and-white with youth
and looks. Our innocence found there no problem

of sweet complicity. The only problem
was how to hold all through one golden summer
the careless posture of our temperate youth.
All our embrace was water in our arms.
Our only summer love was our cold river.
Here lay the fond adventure of the forest.

Our river wore the green sleeves of the forest
that spelled on her slow depth the mirrored problem
of dark green trees reversed upon the river.
We skimmed the calm with flat stones, all that summer,
slung from the sinewy whip of our thin arms.
To carve water was all desire of our youth.

In time of sunset air and the first youth
of evening, shore fires burned before the forest
and all its gloom behind. The bending arms
of swimmers made their rippled wakes a problem
of crossing lines on that midnight midsummer
black-and-gold slippery surface of the river.

And summertime comes back and means the river
and irresponsible grace and careless youth
when we were young and wasted all our summer
and would not see the world beyond the forest,
the adult life to win, the task, the problem,
the angry nations and the globe in arms.

Leave us our time of the river, our time of forest
and green of youth when the world was still no problem
since all that summer we held the world in our arms.